The Equator and Other Disappointments

Trisha Broomfield

First Edition
1st June 2016
ISBN: 978-1-907435-33-1

Published by Dempsey & Windle

Cover Design by Janice Windle
from a painting by Trisha Broomfield

dempseyandwindle.co.uk

15 Rosetrees
Guildford
Surrey
GU1 2H

For J

with love

A Disclaimer

Poems are snapshots
of moments in time
things I daren't say
all wrapped up in rhyme

Poems are dangerous
heart-warming and deep
some of my poems
might send you to sleep

But none of them
                        are about
                                    you

Contents

All Right Together 7
Homeland 9
The Equator and Other Disappointments 10
Down Under 11
My Red Pedal Car 12
The Village School 13
Bobby 14
King of All He Surveys 15
The Hithtory Teacher 16
The Housemistress 17
The Most Beguiling Boy in Louth 18
In my Dreams 20
Kisses 21
Westway 22
March Heatwave 23
The Rusty Steed 24
A Cotswold Sky 26
Purple Paper 27
Virgin Snow 28
Duelling in the Public Bar 29
Time is all Yours 30
The Sunflower Field 31
Ghosts of the Cotswolds 32
Valentine's Flowers 33
'Cope With All' Shoulders 34
Cold Custard 35
The Faded Wilton 36
All White 37
Cattolica 39
If I Met You Tomorrow 40
Books 42
It'll be the Poet's Fault 44

All Right Together

I don’t want to go. Dad says it will be education to go to Australia but I thought that was school. Mum says she has no clothes. But she says it will be all right because we will all be together.

We are here. Mum still has no clothes because it is too hot. I have my own bedroom.

When we have breakfast ants come out and put our sugar puffs onto their shoulders and walk away in single file, mum says they are soldiers.

There is metal cage at the kitchen window to stop the cockroaches. I can hear their armour crack as they try to fly out.

There’s a lizard in my bed mum grabs it by the tail, it runs off and leaves her holding a tail. She says it will grow another one.

I go to a school that is up on stilts. We don’t have milk but different colours of fizzy drinks and straws. Mum has to keep her lipstick in the fridge and there is no chocolate.

There is a swimming pool at school. The changing room walls have tiles the colour of water. I can’t come out of the changing room there is a huge insect blocking my way. I am too scared to jump over it. Mum tells me afterwards it is a praying mantis and won’t bite me.

It is Christmas and people go to the beach. We don’t. We have turkey sandwiches because it is too hot. Dad has bought us a paddling pool. I like it here.

Dad has a cooked breakfast because he is still English and mum gets very hot.

When it floods we paddle in the garden. There are white grubs in the water. The paperboy throws the paper into the garden and dad has to dry it out.

At Easter, there is still no chocolate. My Easter egg is made of pink sugar and is as hard as my teeth.

We have an earthquake, the television wobbles, and the sideboard. It sounds like thunder. There are cartoons on the television.

Mum sings 'It's now or never' and is crying; she wants to stay. We are leaving. I sit on the school bus with presents in a plastic bag. The perfume Harry gave me is in a glass bottle. It breaks and spills over my sweets. I don't want to go but mum says it will be all right because we will all be together.

Homeland

Standing, small feet on the rail
Watching the Indian Ocean froth, curled like butter
By the bow of the Oronsay
Flying fish, then in the distance the crust of a country
Your homeland
Though we would not meet
For another twenty-five years

Warm breeze on skinny bare legs
Quoits on deck
And rusty puddles
Strands of hair always across my face
Clutching at sea salt ice cream
Though it would not be fashionable
For another twenty-five years

Talking at a camera that would never hear my voice
Hiding from Neptune's men as we crossed the Equator
The rocking horse rocking itself
Across The Bay of Biscay
Waiting for you to join me
In our homeland
Waiting for another twenty-five years

The Equator and Other Disappointments

They told me if I watched the water as we crossed the Equator
It would
Flow the opposite way
Down the plughole but it didn't
They told me if I was good when I had my tonsils out
I could have ice cream
But they brought me junket
Have you any idea how that tastes?
They told me if I ate the skin from the fish
I would be brainy
Really
They told me if I ate all the crusts from my toast
I would have curly hair
And if I finished my supper
there would be no starving children
in the world

Down Under

'We used to live there.'
I pointed to the sea level splash of green
on the otherwise buff coastline.
'Really? But it's so far away!'
I shrugged, 'We all went,
the whole family.'
'But even so, thousands of miles.'
I paused in thought
'Yes,' I said 'but nothing changed...
except the lizards in our beds
the ants in the kitchen,
the frog in the cistern
the spiders in our shoes
the cockroaches in the washroom
the horses running loose
the wallabies in the park
the praying mantis in the pool
the kookaburras in the trees
the witchetty grubs in the garden
the black and white moths like tablemats
the hibiscus flowers by the back door...
Oh and our house up on stilts
and mum keeping her lipstick in the fridge,
otherwise it was just the same.'

My Red Pedal Car

I wanted a pedal car
A car that would carry me
Speedily through the garden
From the coal bunker to the rose arch
I could almost feel the wind in my hair
See the dahlias blur as I passed
I wanted a red pedal car

I wanted a pedal car
A red one, I nagged, I pleaded
My parents eventually capitulated
With words of warning which passed
Right over my three year old head
Because I wanted a pedal car
A red one

I wanted a pedal car
And one day there it was
A red one, its paint gleamed
The smile on my face ached
I clambered in,
White socks and Clarks sandals
A soft 'vroom vroom' in my mouth

I wanted a pedal car
A red one
I sat on the metal seat
Feet on the pedals
The 'vroom vroom' getting louder
The words, which had passed over my head
Were repeated 'But you have to pedal it, poppet.'

The Village School

Cloud shadows chase each other
Across the playground
Grey memories
Rise from the tarmac
Children's shouts and laughter
Echo in the void
Images of grazed knees,
Dried tears and loose teeth
The ghosts of parents
Hovering, being bullies and bullied
All over again
There is a constant keening
In the wind
Dandelions do not dare
Disrupt the ground once stamped
By scores of scuffed school shoes

Scaffolding towers above the old school bell
A builder's sign firmly nailed
Smokers take a break
In the playground
Brazen shouts and laughter
Packed lunch, crisps and crumpled news
Snatching sun on patches of tarmac
Dandelions burst through
No longer afraid
Of the headmistress

Bobby

I recall vividly
The smell of your fresh air hair
Your strawberry scented cheeks
The sight of your jam sticky fingers
Mud stained tears that dried before reaching your chin

Then a truck reversing
Sweeping you away in a moment
As though you had never lived

I recall vividly
The blood matting your fresh air hair
Staining your strawberry scented cheeks
Reddening your jam sticky fingers
And the tears dry on my face before reaching my chin

King of all he surveys

Henry wore a crown
Bright yellow cardboard with
Arches, like a child's drawing
I designed a diadem
With poster paint gems, sapphire and ruby
We sat side by side on wooden chairs
The metal legs scraping the stage
While the rest of the class played our subjects

The teacher chose Henry because
He was solid looking
Why she chose me
I will never know
Henry was a kindly king
And fair
I his queen was suitably regal
And looked down my nose a lot

Henry is often on the television
He doesn't look so solid now
But still a kindly man
Beaming at his subjects
From the House of Commons
I suppose he is still a king of sorts, while I
Am not even remotely regal
Though I still look down my nose a lot

The Hithtory Teacher

The hithtory teacher threw chalk
But only at the boys
Occasionally a board rubber would skim
The pert ribbons and ponytails
Thwacking on the back wall of the classroom
Hitting the pink Belgian Congo squarely in the eye

The hithtory teacher dotted all his 'i's and crossed his 't's
But because he talked with a lisp
We learned about
the battle of Marthden Moor
and
the Printhes in the Tower
and
the importanth of the Thpinning Jenny
and
the Aboluthian of Thlavery
whilst watching bethpeckled Thmith
the clath thwot duck the mithiles
thrown
by the hithtory teacher

The Housemistress

Nicotine curls top
smoke wreathed smiles and
dragon teeth
fat flop slippers
dangerously pink
waddling with a swift
turn of speed
silently
along oak creak boards
ignoring tights wrapped round radiator pipes
and Dubonnet in the dressing table

Legs stump down
to her lair
where she has
her own vices
her tipple Campari
with Black Cat chasers
drawn in seconds to an ashy death
hooded lids droop
lips pout and blow
her swimming dreams

She starts awake
heaving from her horse hair sofa
to scale the off piste stairs
and swing the brass hand bell
'Lights out!'
descending again
with slippers sliding
for just one more
night cap

The Most Beguiling Boy in Louth

Bryan had long dark hair
Jenny said like Richard III
She'd seen a painting
I agreed because he always had the hump.
Bryan's eyes were blue, constantly shifting, searching
Never resting on anyone for long
His pale lips flickered
A secret smile

Bryan never spoke
But smoked Gitanes
He drank black coffee
Wore a leather jacket and biker boots
Though we both knew he didn't own a bike.
All the boys wanted to be him
Jenny and I wanted to be with him
But were too scared

Bryan was a legend
His life a mystery
His legs were long and thin like spindly sticks
His moodiness was broodiness
And sixties trendy
Jenny and I thought him the most beguiling boy in Louth
Dangerous like Jason King
Before he was gay

Bryan was a genius, Jenny said
That was why he didn't speak
Disloyal I wondered if he was just thick
Teachers avoided him; even his mother could not cope

Bryan continued to smoke
And fix us with fidgety eyes until one day
He drank Domestos
And his secret smile died.

In My Dreams

In my dreams I wear a dress
Float on heels and swing through life
But when I look down
I see the same old blue jeans

I sit on the tufty grass
My toes scrunch the pebble dashed sand
The sea breeze whips my hair
In strands across my face

I gaze out to sea
And on the horizon you dance
The setting sun gilding your hair
Forever out of reach

In my dreams I wear a dress
Together we swing through life
But my boots are stuck in seashells
The salt stings my face

Kisses

Our kisses were soft
That endless August
And kisses were all we had
Kisses and promises
Born to be broken
At fifteen we owned our world
From the soaring limestone keep
To the grassy moat
Littered with ancient rock
And the supernal sky
Cut only by a kestrel.

Westway

The sun streaks across the Westway
As we thunder along the rise
Riding the colours of the sky

'The Bonneville sounds like a bus!'
I shout to the wind
My words snatched backwards
Out of reach
Guarded eyes catch my smile in the mirror
You nod, having missed my words
And return a gloved thumbs-up.

This is how we communicate
As we ride the colours of the sky
Taking turns
To shout to the wind
And watch our words
Snatched backwards
Out of reach
Guarded smiles searching for signs that all is well
Misunderstanding,
The glue, which binds us together.

March Heatwave

Rooks, Hell's Angels of the sky
Fly chapter tight on silvered wings.
Liquorice sticks of shaded trunks
Black stripe the road ahead
And oaks caught leafless
Stand self-conscious statues
While early blossoms
Exhibit no such shame but
Joyous sway and dance
Caught up in spring's unlikely
Heat haze trance.

The Rusty Steed

My knight in shining armour
Flying down the hill on your rusty steed
Hair blowing wild in the wind
Your summer sky eyes
Bright and keen
A mission on your mind
And honour in your heart
We abandoned the rusty steed
Packed what we could carry,
My silver forks and frying pan
Your darts and football boots,
We took a bus then train
Smiling free as the breeze
Rose tinted glasses firmly in place

Mr. and Mrs., I don't think so,
The receptionist looked as I signed the book
But despite the décor, thirties thrift,
We stayed in paradise, room 212,
Scandalously, hilariously, mini bar emptyingly
Enraptured and in love
While the rusty steed awaited your return, patiently.
Settling the bill the, 'what next?' question
Caught us out
The pay cheque at the end of the month
Was forever away and pub peanuts
Not enough to sustain our love

One morning I caught you
Sideways glancing at my wrinkles
Your summer sky eyes turned to autumn

As dampness drew in and leaves
Fell like tears padding out puddles
Greyness descended and pink champagne
Was merely the colour of the bed-sit bathroom
The piteous whine
Of your neglected rusty steed tugged at your heart strings
Until with a snap
You ran back.

A Cotswold Sky

The dipping sun sets bricks and bark ablaze
Until in wonder at how much fire it can impart
I mention it to others
But then of course
The sky empties in a trice
Now coolest blue with violet
Belies the force with which
The earlier fire seared through
A Cotswold sky
The embers hidden
Until the following day
The fire locked into bricks
And tree trunks
To be released anew
When sinking sunlight
Ignites clay and wood
As though the world around us would combust
And turn to dust

Purple Paper

You wrote me a letter
On purple paper
The words ordered, the thanks sincere
The sentiments expressed
Without sentiment
The emotions restrained,
Trained into neat paragraphs

Reading between the lines
Took me a whole mug of tea
And you, two pages of
Small scrawl the same I had replied to
Aged fifteen, lying belly in the long grass
Sun on my back
While the wood pigeon called

You wrote me a letter
On purple paper, purposeful prose
For a purpose
It was not the ink,
Blue and mature in expression
But the paper, its code rode
Into my heart on the veins of memory
A wood pigeon called
While the sun bathed my back

Virgin Snow

Snowflakes swirl round us
Cherry blossom in the night
The silent thud of lace on lace
They kiss my face,
Melt on my mouth
Tiny perfect parachutes
Tumble and free-fall, twirl and land
Holding hands in your hair
You wear an icy crown

The velvet night is endless
Like our futures
Uncertain and untrodden
Like the snow, falling stars
Caught in amber streetlights
Dancing to their death
Our breath precedes our words
Faces flushed with hope
Confetti on our dreams

Slipping, sliding, breathless, bursting
With love untried and blinded
Joyous in our rush
Laughing, hand holding
You shout my name into the inky night
In the café we steam the windows
Feed the jukebox greedy for our song
My coffee chills
Your eyes shine back with ice

Duelling in the Public Bar

This is the place where my father drank
With his friends from the theatre up the hill
Would be Gielguds duelling in the public bar
Corpsing in the Saloon
The flagstones hold the memory of his footfall
The mirror behind the bar into which he smiled
Leaving a moment of his face
Smiles at me
But that is all

The Far from Madding Crowd hostelry
Is far from isolated now
Expensive vehicles clamour for admittance
As though wishing to hear the echoes
"Time gentlemen please!" and "Ain't you go no 'omes to go to?"
Gone are the dreams.
Wall to wall raised voices
Replace the laughter, the larks.
I try to tell my companions this
They cannot hear me
They smile at me
But that is all

Time Is All Yours

I was always in the shower
The soapiest suds in my hair
My eyes screwed shut
When you phoned
I knew it was you and so
I stomped wet feet to the phone
Arms dripping bubbles
You had no sense of timing
Or was it that time was all yours?
No I couldn't meet
I had X, Y and Z to do
This, that and other important things
With which to fill my day
Where as you, I thought unfairly,
Had all the time in the world

Now there is no chance
That when the phone rings and
I am in the shower
The soapiest suds
Foaming down my shoulders
That it will be you
Asking me to drop X, Y and Z
This, that and the other important things
(Which in your absence mean nothing at all)
And meet

For you have a new life
The miles between us prohibit
Meeting at all
I fill my life with meaningless stuffing
While in the clarity of rarified air
Time is all yours

The Sunflower Field

'Did you know', he said, his face an earnest mask
'That sunflowers shimmy in the moonlight?'
'No, do they really?' she answered naively.
He took her by the hand and led her to the field
Where the sunflowers grew tall together
'Be patient.' he said.
And when the moon rose high
She watched the tall stems sway
The hand-leaves shiver
And the wise heads nod.
Gazing past his shoulder
At the auriferous halos
She wondered at their glow,
While she lay, mesmerised by their dance

As the sun rose
The sunflowers stilled
Their shoulders squared
And the hand-leaves dropped to their sides
Some flowers raised their egg yolk petals to the sky
To avoid meeting her gaze
Others hung their heavy heads in shared shame
While one or two stared blank faced at her
Giving nothing away
But she knew they judged her.
A morning breeze caught the stern green stems
Which stilted swayed
But the dance was over
She sighed, caught once more by his lies

Ghosts of the Cotswolds

Pigs the size of rounded tanks
The smell of pink swill
An angry boar shaking the wooden stall
With his roar
Mud rutted into mountains
For school sandals to climb
Strings of horses
Clopping past the tiny windows
Jockeys perched in country colours
The ghost in the dining room
Which mum would allow through the door first
Whatever she was carrying.

Sitting on the deep sofa
Swinging legs, bored
Watching history in the making
Yuri Gigarin
Oblivious to the tragedy of his life
His death
Me running faster than you
Because I could
Never knowing that one day
I would beg you to wait for me
Yellow stone
Mellow memories
No going back

Valentine's Flowers

I told you not to buy me flowers
Exorbitant I said
You quite agreed, extortionate
Especially if they're red
We're both above such silliness
No need to buy today
St. Valentine's a lame excuse
To force husbands to pay

And so I sit alone
Outside the greyest skies
Regretting my determined stance
My decision was it wise?
For empty stands my crystal vase
Abandoned in the hearth
You didn't have to take my words
Quite so much to heart.

You never listen normally
To what I have to say
Why let my words sink in as deep
Today?

'Cope-with-all' Shoulders

Under the table
My feet dance
While empathy etches into my face
My heart goes out to you
And forgets to return
Watching your heavy head
Sunk into your hands
A shroud of despair
Emanating from cope with all shoulders

Under the table
My fingers tap
Tap, tapping out a tune
The one my feet dance to
While sympathy strains my smile
My heart longs to return
To soar, to sing
But watching your leaden soul sink
Weighs heavy on my cope-with-all shoulders

Cold Custard

I hear your anger
Over the pounding of my heart
As we lie in silence
As thick as cold custard
Each chasing a path
To sleep which will not come
Until the chill of moonlight yields
Reluctantly
To a decisive dawn

The Faded Wilton

'What's that?' he said, pointing to her face
Widening her good eye, she stared at him in disbelief
'What's what?' though she knew
The other eye glinted at him through swollen lids
The burgeoning bruise giving her
A rakish air
'What happened to you?' he said.
Incredulity spread, stunning the smile which, with temerity,
Had begun to creep onto her brave face
'You did that.' the words trembled from her lips
Tumbled onto the faded Wilton
'Me?' now denial was his
'Are you mad?'
'Don't you remember?' she dared
Perhaps she was going mad, she thought
As she recalled his fists, furious and fast
'I'll have him,' he said anger rising
'Tell me, who is it?'
She racked her brains for convincing lies
In the end she said
'I fell. Don't you remember?'
'You want to be more careful, you can't
Go out like that. You'll have to stay in until it fades.'
'Of course.' The words melted,
Joining the others on the once proud Wilton.
She turned to reach for the dustpan and brush
And on her knees swept all the words up
Lest they stay and cause offence.

All White

Let's celebrate, redecorate
We'll cover every wall
Let's start anew, a life review
With pots of Farrow and Ball
Great White I think
Or Wimborne White
Two coats or maybe three
Will be enough to cover up
So no one else can see

We'll start at the top
Of a ladder, I'll hold
While you stab at the walls with
White Tie
The ceiling I've chosen
Great White or perhaps
You'd prefer a little White Lie

Then for a wall
An accent of course
House White I believe will suffice
So our friends can accept
That we're happy, content
We've come clean, maybe Cream,
And wallow in love, like we did
When magnolia reigned

When we've washed all the brushes
We'll sit hand in hand
Peace pervading our space
We'll soak up our room all shadows and depth

With satisfied smirks
And James White
Heroically hiding our gloom

In a white room that once had its
Passion along with its turbulent shades
When things are All White
Will we be all right?
Or so starved of colour
Our feelings so blanched
That each wall will return to Up Tight

[White Lie and Up Tight are not, to my knowledge, Farrow and Ball shades]

Cattolica

Italian papas in skimpy white swimwear
Dark eyed mamas in headscarves
Beach towels carpeting the softest sand
Learning to say 'guten morgen' and 'guten tag'
Someone shouting at their toddler 'Massimo! Massimo!
The smell of Ambre Solaire
Olive oil and sophisticated lemon wedges
And of breaded veal every meal

The sun bronzing our bodies
And blistering our English rose shoulders
Barry Ryan imploring
Eloise from transistor radios
Fiat 500s spilling boys from
Peeled back sunroofs
Shouting 'Babi! Babi!'
Cattolica, a world away
From Cleethorpes

If I Met You Tomorrow

If I met you tomorrow
I would be yesterday
My legs long and loose
Would whoosh past in flares
I'd walk like a stork in high heels of cork
My hair auburn silk
Would sweep past my shoulders
And my boobs would be where they used to be.
If I met you tomorrow

If I met you tomorrow
You would be yesterday
Your long hair sunshine
Your earring would glint
Your hard body glisten
And you would listen
While your sparkly grey eyes
Devoured me and your lips kissed my lip gloss all off
If I met you tomorrow

If I met you tomorrow
We would be yesterday
Your hand would gently touch my cheek
We'd speak and smile
Revealing teeth recently paid for
And crows' feet would crinkle
Least mine would
In your profession, Botox would hinder their freedom to dance
If I met you tomorrow

If I met you tomorrow
I would be wild and free
In my yesterday dreams
My jeans would not burst at the seams
But would hold your attention
And you would mention in passing
How you'd like to see more
If I met you tomorrow

If I met you tomorrow
All our yesterdays would rush up and haunt us
They would shake hands and embarrass us
Mightily. My dimples would deepen
Your hairline would hide
As you tired to pretend, you were just irresistible
I still love you of course, yesterday, but not
If I met you tomorrow.

Books

Books were once the attraction
And words, which lay therein
Scattered with abandon and joy
On fragile foxy pages
Bringing comfort,
A friendly watchful eye
And the smell
Of frankincense

Your room, a real fire with added flames,
Where we lay too hot to touch
Cocooned in a forest
Of hard covers and spines
While shadows grew
On purple walls
And we sang imprisoned by damp books
Of warped wisdom

I still buy books
Stack my shelves with their
Parental guidance and dry humour
The comfort they offer
Is sterile and the words
Have arranged themselves
Into adult sentences
How dull

The aura of otherworldliness
Has been lost,
The dream magic
Vanished along with the dream
My house has no real fire, no flames

No shadows dance
On magnolia walls
I am alone with my memories

I think of you
At this change of seasons time
When the air sharpens and
Sunlight mellows
While autumn leaves drop,
Dampening to cloth of gold in puddles
And conkers are split
By heavy hurrying boots

Do you still live
In book-lined rooms
And breathe in frankincense
Watching shadows grow on purple walls
And think of me?
I must read a book one day
Instead of thinking
I can write one.

First published in Roundyhouse Magazine

It'll be the Poet's Fault

Try not to write about yourself
Refrain from flowery phrase
Choose adjectives in common use
Leave Roget on the shelf
Or folk will Google all your words
And look up every one
Sidetracked they'll loose all sense of time
View vague celebrities online
Drift off to Amazon and order
Games and then become a hoarder
They'll forget that long before delivery
Next day ensured,
That they had picked up your poem
Being bored
And if you'd kept to simple-speak
They'd not have parted with a week
Of salary saved for paying rent
But on these useless items spent
It'll be the poet's fault
In the end

Trisha Broomfield writes poetry, flash fiction, short stories and unfinished crime novels. Her early influences include the Liverpool poets, Ted Hughes and Thomas Hardy. She creates ceramic figures which threaten to take over the house, produces bizarre drawings, which she sells as cards, and has recently taken up life drawing.

Trisha was born in Lincolnshire and lived in Australia as a child, travelling with her family by boat through the Suez Canal to and from Down Under. Now she lives in Surrey with her husband and shares an irascible cat. Some of her poems have been published in the Welsh literary magazine *Roundyhouse*.

www.ingramcontent.com/pod-product-compliance
Ingram Content Group UK Ltd.
Pitfield, Milton Keynes, MK11 3LW, UK
UKHW041834200726
13854UKWH00003BA/1121